THE PEACEFUL PENCIL

MINDFUL
COLOURING

75 RELAXING PATTERNS TO ENJOY

PEONY PRESS

Relax and unwind with this stress-relieving colouring book of floral patterns. The art of colouring is a form of meditation, focusing the mind and stilling the endless mental chatter that saps our energy and causes stress and negative feelings. As you start to colour in these meditative artworks you will unleash your inner creativity and find yourself gradually moving to a more peaceful and calming state of mind.

You can colour in as little or as much as you like, taking your time to develop your picture the way you want it. There are no hard and fast rules, you are truly free to create your own unique designs whether you choose pencils, pens or paints. Start colouring today and enjoy the still, quiet voice of calm this soothing practice will bring you.

MINDFULNESS IS SIMPLY BEING AWARE OF WHAT IS
HAPPENING RIGHT NOW WITHOUT WISHING IT WERE
DIFFERENT; ENJOYING THE PLEASANT WITHOUT
HOLDING ON WHEN IT CHANGES (WHICH IT WILL);
BEING WITH THE UNPLEASANT WITHOUT FEARING IT
WILL ALWAYS BE THIS WAY (WHICH IT WON'T).

JAMES BARAZ

INNER PEACE CAN BE REACHED ONLY WHEN WE
PRACTICE FORGIVENESS. FORGIVENESS IS LETTING
GO OF THE PAST, AND IS THEREFORE THE MEANS
FOR CORRECTING OUR MISPERCEPTIONS.

GERALD G. JAMPOLSKY

SILENCE IS NOT THE ABSENCE OF SOMETHING
BUT THE PRESENCE OF EVERYTHING.

ANONYMOUS

WE HAVE FORGOTTEN WHAT ROCKS AND
PLANTS STILL KNOW – WE HAVE FORGOTTEN HOW
TO BE – TO BE STILL – TO BE OURSELVES – TO BE
WHERE LIFE IS HERE AND NOW.

ECKHART TOLLE

NOTHING CONTRIBUTES SO MUCH TO TRANQUILIZE
THE MIND AS A STEADY PURPOSE.

MARY SHELLEY

THE MOMENT ONE GIVES CLOSE ATTENTION TO
ANYTHING, EVEN A BLADE OF GRASS, IT BECOMES
A MYSTERIOUS, AWESOME, INDESCRIBABLY
MAGNIFICENT WORLD IN ITSELF.

HENRY MILLER

TIME, LIKE LIFE ITSELF, HAS NO INHERENT MEANING.
WE GIVE OUR OWN MEANING TO TIME, AS TO LIFE.

JONATHAN LOCKWOOD HUIE

THE MEETING OF TWO ETERNITIES,
THE PAST AND THE FUTURE...
IS PRECISELY THE PRESENT MOMENT.

HENRY DAVID THOREAU

NATURE DOES NOT HURRY,
YET EVERYTHING IS ACCOMPLISHED.

LAO TZU

THE ONLY ZEN YOU FIND ON THE TOPS OF
MOUNTAINS IS THE ZEN YOU BRING UP THERE.

ROBERT M. PIRSIG

LIFE IS A GREAT AND WONDROUS MYSTERY,
AND THE ONLY THING WE KNOW THAT WE HAVE
FOR SURE IS WHAT IS RIGHT HERE AND
RIGHT NOW. DON'T MISS IT.

LEO BUSCAGLIA

When we are unable to find tranquillity
within ourselves, it is useless to
seek it elsewhere.

Francois de la Rochefoucauld

TENSION IS WHO YOU THINK YOU SHOULD BE.
RELAXATION IS WHO YOU ARE.

CHINESE PROVERB

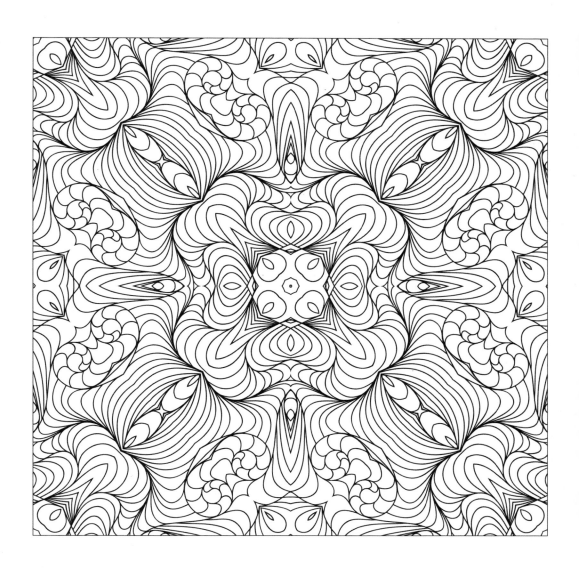

LOOKING AT BEAUTY IN THE WORLD, IS THE
FIRST STEP OF PURIFYING THE MIND.

AMIT RAY

Life isn't about waiting for the storm to pass.
It's about learning to dance in the rain.

Anonymous

GOING BACK TO A SIMPLER LIFE
IS NOT A STEP BACKWARD.

YVON CHOUINARD

FOR MANY YEARS, AT GREAT COST, I TRAVELLED
THROUGH MANY COUNTRIES, SAW THE HIGH
MOUNTAINS, THE OCEANS. THE ONLY THINGS I DID
NOT SEE WERE THE SPARKLING DEWDROPS IN
THE GRASS JUST OUTSIDE MY DOOR.

RABINDRANATH TAGORE

WRITE IT ON YOUR HEART THAT EVERY DAY
IS THE BEST DAY IN THE YEAR.

RALPH WALDO EMERSON

THIS EDITION IS PUBLISHED BY PEONY PRESS
AN IMPRINT OF ANNESS PUBLISHING LTD,
108 GREAT RUSSELL STREET, LONDON WC1B 3NA;
INFO@ANNESS.COM

WWW.ANNESSPUBLISHING.COM;
TWITTER: @ANNESS_BOOKS

IMAGES COURTESY OF SHUTTERSTOCK